About the Author

Ty Smith is a new author, with *Here to Stay (An Anthology)* as his first literary work. He enjoys writing poetry, traveling frequently, playing guitar, and using time to connect with the people he loves. Music—whether listening to it or playing it—is his lifeline. With his friends, he typically travels the world to watch some of his favorite artists perform. He currently resides in Houston, TX.

Here to Stay (An Anthology)

Ty Smith

Here to Stay (An Anthology)

Olympia Publishers
London

www.olympiapublishers.com
OLYMPIA PAPERBACK EDITION

Copyright © Ty Smith 2024

The right of Ty Smith to be identified as author of
this work has been asserted in accordance with sections 77 and 78 of
the Copyright, Designs and Patents Act 1988.

All Rights Reserved

No reproduction, copy or transmission of this publication
may be made without written permission.
No paragraph of this publication may be reproduced,
copied or transmitted save with the written permission of the publisher,
or in accordance with the provisions
of the Copyright Act 1956 (as amended).

Any person who commits any unauthorised act in relation to
this publication may be liable to criminal
prosecution and civil claims for damage.

A CIP catalogue record for this title is
available from the British Library.

ISBN: 978-1-83543-038-5

This is a work of fiction.
Names, characters, places and incidents originate from the writer's
imagination. Any resemblance to actual persons, living or dead, is
purely coincidental.

First Published in 2024

Olympia Publishers
Tallis House
2 Tallis Street
London
EC4Y 0AB

Printed in Great Britain

Dedication

To Anita,
You motioned for freedom, longed to love, and told me all about your dreams.
Now here I am to hold them to my heart until my time to go home is nigh.
Thank you for being a friend.

Acknowledgments

A fever dream. This is what this anthology is to me. I spent years of my life as a flight attendant writing poems on random hotel notepads, most of which ended in heartache. My rule was to never check out of my hotel room until I had written a poem that made me feel safe, or rather, a poem that paid homage to my emotions in that specific period of my life. To this day, I still have most of the poems in this anthology on the original written paper from said notepads. Knowing they are captured here, along with several other personal poems, makes this book worth every sleepless night. To say that I put this together on my own would be futile. I would like to thank specific people in my life who did more than raise me as their village child.

To Nick and Stephanie, my parents in the sky. Thank you so much for your never-ending love and devotion to my craft(s). Your unwavering spirits have given me hope in places I thought I would stay in forever. Ever since that day, I wounded up on your three-day trip, I knew something was going to transpire, but no one told me it would be for a lifetime. I wouldn't change it for the world. Above all, thank you for inspiring me to wield my power. This is me doing just that. Let's get McDonald's soon.

To B.B., my moon, there are no words to express my gratitude for you. Those nights you saw me cry over something I knew I could not fix. The times you worried for me, wondering if I was okay. For moments like hot springs when you knew how I felt:

thank you. Thank you for spending every waking moment pushing me to do something more with this art. Thank you for showing me that there are connections to be made in this world and that people are longing to be heard. I hope that I make you proud for how I am helping bridge those gaps. We all deserve to be seen and heard. I am doing my best, and this is me trying.

To everyone who read my works in their early cocoon stages along with my botched manuscript: Jorge, Lola, Squid, Dallas, Jennifer, Destin, Heather, and to anyone else that took time out of their life to read this anthology. You all are the nicest critics anyone could have asked for. Thank you a million times over.

To Carter for being the best Barb in the Barb army. And to EEEEMAH for keeping a smile on my face just by saying "CLEOR?"

To MUNA, the greatest musicians of all time, who gave me an umbrella in my fiercest storms: Thank you for being the loudspeaker that so many like myself needed in our lives. You helped me find security in my art, my love, and my dreams. You were right: It's Gonna Be Okay, Baby.

To the select few that inspired me for so many of these poems: thank you for being so authentic in who you are. Whether you know it or not, you have given me the greatest gift by sharing your stories with me, or allowing me to be a part of your journey (vice versa). What is more, you have made me wiser by teaching me the difference between what I want and what I deserve. Where there was once hate, there now thrives love, and I wish you all so much of it forevermore.

To the publishing team at Olympia Publishers: thank you for taking a chance on a sad boy. All the patience you accumulated for me is sweeter than the finest honey. I wish I could throw you all a party for just being that amazing with me. Your opportunity has allowed me to flourish in ways I only used to dream about. Here is to a bright future and many more poems because of you.

To all my parents: each moment of time has been monumental for all of us. This anthology stands as a fine example of what you have achieved. These works are dedicated to you for allowing me to be here on this planet and for always giving me the shove I needed in order to go in the right direction (although the beaten path was fun sometimes).

My love is with you always, to the moon and back.

To anyone else in my life who has held me up in support whenever I fall short—specifically the wiser ones: You are never unnoticed, and I think of you frequently and fondly. My heart is forever stamped with the impressions that you have made on me. I hope that this anthology makes you proud.

Lastly, to anyone out there in the world hoping for a signal: This beacon is for you. You are not alone, you are never alone. I hope somewhere in this anthology that you find the shards of hope hidden beneath the letters. Thank you for reaching out. This moment might seem hard, but it is not impossible. The humanistic pains we suffer are only temporary. This, too, will pass. You are stronger than you know. Please give yourself that credit. Never give up, and never quit. No matter who you are, just know that someone, somewhere, loves you.

Table of Contents

Intolerable 15
Is This Giving up or Giving In? 16
Little Green 17
Hiding in Plain Sight 18
The Muse 19
Who I Am 21
The Shift 22
The Superiority Complex Monster 23
I Love It. 23
Blank Pages 24
Reflective Respite 25
Body 26
Ode to a Season 27
The Dream of Forgiveness 28
Stripped 29
Song, Song, Song 30
Anita 31
Holes 33
Shower Promises 34
To Be No One 35
Here to Stay 37
Christmas Hopes 38
Tell Me I'm Not the Only One 39
Morning, How Soon I Forget 40
Boxed Dreams 41

Stone Wishes	42
Man, Lady, and Me	43
A Note Left in Paris Just for You	45
Twenty-Eight Peaces of Me	46
I Need It	47
Lantern Nights	49
Pine Tree Cells	50
No Destination	51
With Time…	52
In the Dark	53
Running Riot	54
The Apology	55
Hike Views	57
Pella Tulips	59
Patience	61
Summer's Memento of You	62
Out the Seattle Window	63
Overboard	64
The Season I Loved You	65
Light of My Life	68
Moon to Me	69
Trees	70
Re: Nothing	72
A Motet to Fear	73
Little Long Hair	74
Hot Springs	75

Intolerable

Intolerable. I can get intolerable. But everything around me is just as intolerable.
Irritating is what they are.
I'm sick of the annoyance everything brings me.
Stop with how fake you are.
I'm not just talking about you, I'm talking about me too.
Here I lay irritated, left naked in a towel on the floor, picking at my skin wondering. "What's next? What's next? What's next?" Haven't showered in a day. I'm seeped in yesterday's memories.
Isn't that just intolerable?

Is This Giving up or Giving In?

Nobody tells you getting older,
Makes you colder
And life's about what you do,
Not what you don't.
But I'm too tired to think,
So I won't
complain about the little things.
When everything is killing me
I'm going down now.
Are you feeling me?
Are you feeling me?

Little Green

Little Green, Big Dreams
Small weeds, poison feeds,
But still he grows.
Yes, he's a Little Green
With a gentle reach
For the sun.
Little Green for a color to shine.
Oh, Little Green, you are mine.
Little Green holds life
Where thanks and love fall short
Little Green, you are adored.
Little Green, Big Dreams,
No weeds, just flowers,
And he still grows.

Hiding in Plain Sight

This journey will be a very long one. Sometimes I think it will never end. When I die, I hope I can recollect all that I did for me.

Until then, I am hiding. Running along a path only I can go down. But if the fates are kind, maybe I'll see you on the other side of it!
I hope we don't recognize each other. I hope it is like meeting people with the vessels of the old, but the souls of the new. This is what I desire most.

I am hiding. And in truth I don't want you to find me in the eyes of the world. *No.*

I want you to find me, but behold me with the sight that is only yours. Solely yours. Plain sight.

The Muse

So it goes.
There are visits I don't care for.
An unwelcome guest walks through the door.
He claims house and home.
He takes all of it and makes it his own.

He is my demon, He is my muse, tell me what I am going to do
With or without you?

His reign of treachery begins with a mirror
As he fashions it left and right.
Makes me look
Holding my eyes deep with hooks.
All the terror, all the fright.

He is my demon, He is my muse, tell me what I am going to do
With or without you?

I could try to kill him, trust me I would.
But then, what…?
Tell me I'm not good
Enough…of
This could do the trick.

Self-doubt is a trip.
If you want to die, you should give him a try.

He is my demon, He is my muse, tell me what I am going to do With or without you?

Who I Am

That's just who I am. A little human melted in the mix.
Seeping through the cracks.
Yeah, that's just who I am.
Imperfect but I stay here for you.
Run when I want.
Return when I need.
Never too far.
Yeah, I'm faulting wiring,
But that's just who I am.

The Shift

I feel this shift and it's pulling me away. It drags me like marmalade across the
surface, stripping crumbs of my love for you bit by bit.
Every little piece I can hold on to is all that I will get.

These fractions that I have are only the part of a whole of what used to be.
Now what do I do?

Tears fall to my hands. Tears make it all clear. I'm so confused. All I can do is wash away the years of our memories, yet I am forced to choose.

The final turn comes and I must grab on again, but the shift pulls me further apart, and I slip from my grip like oil.

Goodbye.

The Superiority Complex Monster

This superiority complex monster: oh, what a beast.
It tickles me to think people assume me to be sweet whenever I hate most things I see.
I desire to stay humble. I wear my self-righteousness like a good pious boy. Oh Lord, bless me.
But ever in the shadows of my heart he creeps…

And I love him. I love him.
I love how he wanders the trees of my aorta.
I love how he reminds me that he's there
I love how he says, "You are better. You are beyond worthy. More worthy than anyone else…better than them."

I Love It.

I beg him to take me away. Make me the monster that you are.
I don't want to be weak anymore. Maybe it is better to be feared than to be loved. Only he would know.
Slowly I reach for his claws that long to peel me to the core…
but I hesitate and pull away.

He is there, I am here.
Both of us are waiting.

Blank Pages

Everyday I'm gonna see things like a blank page. Yeah, I'm gonna turn the new leaf whenever I want. I'm bound by the same book until death do me part, but you can't hold me to the same story!

I'll write my way to a new adventure whenever the call comes.

Hello, Reader, I'm glad you came! Thank you for watching this character grow.

Blank pages wavering, waiting for me to spill my secrets. How safe I feel. Where do I begin? Paper to Pen? Pen to Paper?

Pen to Paper is the hardest. Just to start is the hardest. But there is no 'When.' 'When' is now. 'When' is whenever you want it to be, and *'When' is always right.* That is what you must feel in your heart.

I'm so grateful for these blank pages.

Reflective Respite

I forget how often unexpected moments can help me thrive.
I don't want to live on a whim, but I don't mind
Being whimsical.

That's what helps me the most.
That's where I find myself more and more.

Like this coffee in my hand,
I think I'll sip it
Slowly.

Body

Demons and ghosts of my body haunt me every day.
Perceptions only I see make me feel like I don't belong.

Why is there so much hair?
Am I really that fat?
Why does my stomach do that?

Maybe if I'm lucky enough, the pitch forks they carry will gut me so badly that I lose it all!

Let it burn in the hellfire hearth, because you know what they say:
They, all want their pound of flesh.

Well, I have one hundred and ninety-five pounds they can have. *Freely.*

Ode to a Season

Oh yes, I can feel her creeping on me slowly. She sets upon me like the dawn. I know she's coming, love. She used to kiss me so sweetly. Gently she would embrace me, offering me nothing but freedom. Never has she forsaken me.

With whom does she come with? I do not know. Every year is different. However, all are welcome, as long as she shows up! I can feel her aura. I do not fear her this time. I am ready. I am at my porch with a greeting party.
Hello summer, my old love.

The Dream of Forgiveness

Forgiveness showers us like water to the land.
I knew it when I woke from my dream. I woke in peace.
I knew that you forgave me. I knew that somewhere out in this world
You were thinking of me too.
You are so much more than the fury and hate that we harbor.

Better than that:
You are loved.

Stripped

I'm still haunted by all that went down. But I'm most frightened by the good memories. These are the most dangerous, because as I try to let go they keep hooks in me just to pull me back. I'm lying to myself everyday if I say I'm okay—because I'm not. I say, "I don't need someone, I *want* someone." But that is not true. *I need someone,* and I need them to survive. I am defeated. I want and need because I know I can't do this on my own.

All this to say that they fit the narrative only I created.

I feel lost.

I think I shed my old skin every day and leave it behind. Now I am running naked through the wilderness searching for refuge.

God help me.

I'm vulnerable.

Song, Song, Song

Through this heat,
I see mirages. All the dust blows into my eyes. Oh how the
Sun is so high.
Can you feel its beams the same way I do?
Different places, same sky.
Same sun.
Same moon.

Reflections of myself
Through a sky of storms.
Song, Song, Song, is what I sang before I was born.
This is happiness.
This is forevermore.

Anita

Lilac is a good color for you / Seagulls caw when you
Smile and watch / Soft serve and sprinkles was
Your favorite time / A stop at the beach to feel the
Wind / What I'd give to do it again.

Oh, how you sleep
Oh, how I cried
Oh, how you'd drink your coffee every time.

I'm glad you came / Will you stay the night? / I said yes, not to fret this time.

Oh, how you love me, oh how you cared,
Oh, now you're gone, I wish you were here.

Diet Coke, Never Sprite / The getaways for burger nights/
Horror movies for Christmas frights / All the gossip under
Kitchen lights.

These things I know because of you / Little joys are more than few / Watching planes / And paw prints too / What I'd give to be with you.

Oh, how you sleep
Oh, how I cried

Oh, how you'd drink your coffee every time
I'm glad you came, will you stay the night?
I said yes, not to fret this time.

Oh, how you love me
Oh, how you cared
Now you're gone, I wish you were here.

The tulips that were talked about / The empty chair that sits on its own/
An empty room all alone/
Lilac was such a pretty color for you.

Did you know?

Did you know?

Holes

Here is a hole left by a love that
I lost.
Here is a hole left by the abandoned feelings of a parent.
Here is a hole left by the death of a loved one. My first friend.

Now what?

Snared and trapped, I have fallen deep within. Just when I climb out
of one, I fall back into another.
There I stay weeping, bleeding.
Maybe these holes are where I belong? Will I ever get out?

Here is a hole where my heart once used to beat. Long-live the memory of requited love. Never will you be forgotten.

Here is the hole that I choose to die in.

Savior? I need none.

Shower Promises

I write silent dreams on
Shower walls, with heavy
Heat and steam. All the
Things I'd hope, love, and dream to see.

Slowly, each has come true.
Slowly, each leads me.

I won't give up.

I'll keep my shower promises, even if no one knows, because they matter.
With each stroke of my finger, their
droplet trails fall true.

Maybe shower promises can work for you too?

To Be No One

I know it is what it is, but what I want isn't always what I get.
And moving forward is futile
But it's always the same in the end
And I'm left with none.
Say less. It's done. I'm no one.

Nice to meet you! This is your...who?
Oh, how fun.
It's done. I'm no one.
I know it is what it is, but what I want isn't always what I get.

Maybe if I plan a little harder, work a little faster, change myself a little deeper, they'll see me as someone.
But no matter, it's done. I'm no one.

Okay, one more time. I'll give it another go.
This has to be different, not the same bloke.
Things are going great. I'm feeling as warm as the sun. This is right.
Oh, this could be the one!
Wait, why did you turn the tables?
Did I do something wrong?
Am I not enough?
Is it done?
I thought I was someone? What is happening? Why are you

tearing me down piece by piece? Saying things like, "You have no principles or morales, none!"

All of the love we had lost in just a month.
Our temple, demolished
As quick as it begun
It is finished. It is done.

I know it is what it is, but what I want isn't always what I get.

Here to Stay

Hungry, but I won't eat.
Thirsty, but I won't drink.
Falling into old patterns once
again. I can't seem to
find myself. I'm lost in
the Labyrinth.
Light, oh light,
Won't you
Find me?

Christmas Hopes

Is it Cliche to want to
Believe in the spirit of Christmas?

For all that it's worth, I will.
And to you that I write—
What once would have been the words of past are now words of hope.
So with that spirit, I will begin to *Hope*. Hope will be my gift to
myself, to you, and to my future so abundant.

Merry Christmas.

Tell Me I'm Not the Only One

The questions I've been asking
Lately, have all been for myself.
And I wonder, are the answers
Something I need to hear or am
Am I lying about those too?

I feel so much like an
Imposter for all that I do. I just can't help but think though,
Maybe everyone else does too?

Morning, How Soon I Forget

Lying in the night might
Bring certain sadness,
But the morning keeps its
Promise.
Joy, you are
Welcomed here.
Take my hand.
Kiss my head.
Lead me to your peace.

Boxed Dreams

Here I sit with just a box
and a dream.

So many days I shake it
And I reach in but
Can't seem to get a hold of my dreams.
I want to stop dreaming.
I want to start being.

Boxed dreams kept on display.
Always there—but to my dismay, I fail.
Just another dream.

A fraud like a fool with a scheme.

Oh, God, just give me my dreams…
Please.

Stone Wishes

Lichen suppressed my ancestors
As did the material before them.
Hand in hand they worked.

Blood, sweat, and tears built them
In this very spot for their prayers.

But here I am dangling high toward
The sun with a thousand wishes to
offer.

No wind can move me that isn't from your body.
Stone wishes are waiting for you my love.

So pick me, make me your own, and
I promise you the world.

Send me away.
My stone wishes are yours.

Man, Lady, and Me

What a strong man, with individual strength
To carry the world on his back
Without a complaint.
Such a strong man.
A warrior to see. I'd kill to be like him
But I'm just too weak.

She's a fine lady,
Everyone loves her.
A killer bee to some,
A beauty to others
Such a fine lady.

They're two of the same
Amateurs in a game-
Then they made me.
I just wanna change
I don't want their habits
I don't want their ways
I wanna be different
I'm gonna break the chain.

The sins of your fathers were not yours
I wish I could help, I know you hate each other.

And no matter how much I beg
No matter how much I cry
You could never love again even if you tried.

I'm your son
I'm your little bubba
I'm your Ty.

I'm your son
I'm your little bubba
I'm your Ty.

A Note Left in Paris Just for You

I came to Paris looking for reasons
To believe in something beyond me.
I tried going to a book shop where
I told a girl to read Dante and Milton
Hoping to find direction in a poetry book that I hadn't heard of.

I came to Paris with memories of the things you said. Of all the places you used to go to. Now you're not here and it's a city with big towers and ghost palaces.
May the Sun King's rays shine over my dreary hopes of being with you again.

I came to Paris and I cried in the night. I didn't tell my two friends because I wanted them to know I was all right without killing a good time.

I came to Paris and no dreams came true.
I'm still in Paris hoping to find you.

Twenty-Eight Peaces of Me

I've been doing some thinking lately,
Alot about peace really.
And when I think about peace,
I think about how there is a reclaiming of your own power.
This power may have been stolen from you,
It may have been dormant,
Or it may have died.
No matter what happened to it, your power is yours once you choose peace.

I've been doing some thinking lately about peace, and I think
I'm choosing confidently to keep it,
Wielding it as my own.

I Need It

I want to rip this shirt off
Scrap this tie
Tear this vest
I need to cut loose
Come free
I'm ready to be a freak
I'm ready to move
To embrace the abnormalities
Yeah, you can look
Hell, I don't care if you touch
But I get to touch you right back
Look at me like that again
I love the way you do it.
These eyes were made to kill
Papa gave them to me
Grade A, sweet as can be
Let me show you what I got
I'm young and only for so long
So let me move to my own song
Before they turn these lights off.
It's primal
It's feral
Touch me
Bite me
Punch

Kick
Scream
Whatever you want
It's happening.
Yeah, my time is now
Do me
Over
And over
And over Again.

Lantern Nights

Littler Lantern raise your hands to the skies
I pushed you there so high
I wanted new things to come from your departure
I cried and smiled
I prayed to you and whispered,
"Bring me new dreams."
You floated on.
So bright you glistened in the night sky.
There you were with all your friends
They too carried the dreams of the masses below.
How many of those dreams came true?
Onward, you went for what seemed like a millennium.
And what I saw was a sea of stars that I could touch.
So I did.
I wanted to reach up and hold your flame close to my heart.
Dust covered boots on desert grounds. Giddy up cowboy hats from above.
You saw it all, you my little lantern with words tattooed to your sides.

You float on forever in my heart, in my dreams.

Pine Tree Cells

Out my window, there are pine trees.
They sway in the summer morning sun
I sit stable in this hotel room
Trapped knowing it's not his fault.
He's just a room.
He's just doing his job.
My friend told me yesterday that he read what I wrote
He said, I was angry. I told him, he was right
How else am I supposed to be when I'm broken?
I loved the sound of it all though.
"Write a book," he said.
I'm going to.
This prison isn't so bad.
I'll keep doing what I do.
My little spoon I use to dig will get me out of this cell eventually.
It's been passed down to me by others
And they're telling me it's my turn for freedom.
Hold tight because I'll be there soon.

The coffee has finished.
Cheap, cheap, coffee, but I'll drink it anyway.
I'm not ungrateful.
I like those pine trees outside
Their green brings me the hope I seek in all the little things in my life.

No Destination

I wanted to see you
I drove to meet you
Knew you didn't want to
Now I'm stuck feeling numb too.
Quick drive down the Avenue
Out of the way but I'll come to you
Beck and call, I'm yours so true
A situation-ship in between far and few.
Together finally only to bid adieu
How much more can I take
Just to hear the words 'I love you?'

With Time...

Bottom of the fridge
Back of the class
Always forgotten
Always last.

One day, something changed.

Now top of the brass
All things of the past
This is what time can
Do for those who love and grow so vast.

In the Dark

I sit here in a daze
Thinking of ways to turn a phrase
Flushed from drinking myself down the drain.
When the party's over
When the beds are made
I can't think of anything else in the dark
Only your face.

Running Riot

Running riot I find
That time cannot hold me
But running riot keeps me going.
And if I never stop,
Well, I guess in the end
Time wins
Because then
All I ever did was
Run riot.

The Apology

In the turn of events,
A lie meant to spare
The expense of your feelings
Turns out coming back around
To stab you right in the back,
Straight to the heart.
And when you bleed into your hands
All I can do is say, "I'm sorry." And walk away.
As if that helps,
With just a band aid to patch it all up.
I couldn't bare it
So I continue going and I say I'll come back,
When truthfully, I stay in the woods of my self-punishment.
What you don't know is that
I returned the tickets I had bought because I knew it was what
I needed to do.
No, please don't argue with me over it.
It is done. I would be tortured every second on the floor
knowing what I did.
So I did what I had to do.
And in my head all I could hear was my father yelling at me
For the things I had done wrong.
"A liar stays in the liar room!" he screams.
So I go. And I sit on the bed, knees folded, and I look through
the threshold with no door. There in the room across the hall

stands the ghost of you
staring at me with those eyes saying,
"How could you be Judas when you knew?"
So I am here writing.
I said I would only return when I had an apology worthy of saying more than sorry.
I hope you know that I cannot understand why I lied. I was so scared of saying to you
that I wanted to experience something on my own. I reached deep into the safety of my memory and took out the music of someone who protected me through my childhood, and paying homage to them alone was more important than us.
I see now how selfish that can be.
Instead of being patient, I neglected the conversation we had for the rushed safety and thrill of the experience.
More importantly, I was willing to sacrifice a house of trust we built in order to secure myself in a trailer of trash. To some this is minor, to me this is our house going up in smoke.
After all, one little spark causes a flame.
And for what? Two hours of sound that can be repeated with a push of a button?
Tours happen all the time. Like a circle, young man Adam will come around. I'll catch him again.
I was blinded by greed
By insecurity
By anger
For this, I apologize.
In your time, in your delicate time,
I hope you can forgive me.
That nocturnal city won't be forever,
But our friendship will.
You are loved dearly.

Hike Views

Hike views from
On top of the hill.

The Fresh breeze hitting
My restart button and
Deleting the back logs of worry.

On Malibu sunsets,
Favored lovers
In the heart of
Time stopping with you.

Can you feel it? The heartbeat
Of what I would do to love you?

The dreams of the sea keep me
At bay here in your arms
Like a lost ship coming to the shore.

Being So high on these feelings
And so high on the cliff
Is all so new to me.

I breathe in my luck- thinking of my unlucky
Inexperienced youth.

But who cares?

God what a hike.

I love this view.

I love you.

Pella Tulips

Whisked hair, jet black from the days before she knew who she was getting during those pick-up truck nights.
And she spoke of tulips in Pella, Iowa, like they were keys to her freedom.

The dandelion Polaroids said it all: She missed those days full of smiles. Now she just smokes and watches him kill himself slowly.

How many guests sat at his table when she wasn't around?
She knew—she always knew.

She still dreamed of Pella tulips every night.

The only bargaining she can do is with someone she can't see.
"Please bring him home to me," she says.
And so he comes home,
Tainted with Busch creeping in the winds of his breath, but
He returns nonetheless like a rental trashed from the drive.

Still, she daydreams of Pella tulips, All the colors blossoming
In the sun.

Softly, the cigarette is flicked
Deeply, the cough is had.

She keeps her vows, for the sake of loyalty, because that's who
She is.
So she lights another one and says,
"Why do I put up with this?"

In that haze and heat of a Texas sky, she sits on her porch and
Closes her eyes.

Dreaming again in technicolor of only Pella tulips, and with
Outreached hands eternally young,
She plucks one.
Softly, she kisses its satin edges.

There she stays in the war of colors planted deep in her
memory.

She is home forever.

Patience

When my back's against the wall
And there's nothing I can do,
I'll choose to sit quietly and watch.
But just know I'm sharpening my ax
While I wait.

And when the time is right,
I'll take my swing.
Don't ever say you never saw it coming
Because karma is swift and powerful.
She knocked on your door and you left her in the rain.
Now, she is home.
I can wait patiently.

Summer's Memento of You

The clock on my wall ticks and I think to myself how I'd love a cup of coffee. Staying up all night wasn't on my agenda, especially if I couldn't do it with you.
I reflect over my summer and the memories I made.
Long days fighting back invisible heat waves, forever laughing through drunken stupors.
My friends cured the disease left by love. I'll thank them later.

I'm on this couch, huddled under a blanket, writing a letter I'll never send. In those summer memories, you weren't there, yet every day you showed up.
Riddle me that.

Out the Seattle Window

The French hair spray
A little forte
And they say
There will be
Some days like this,
When it feels this fog won't lift.
Well, what if it never does?
What if the solar winds never blow them
To someone else's dreary day?
I wonder.

Overboard

Then time sailed our boats into a sea
Where the wind blew our sails in opposite directions.
But if you said the word, I'd swim to you
through any flotsam and jetsam
From our storms left behind.

The Season I Loved You

I wake in the night with dreams of you,
I never know if they're okay to have.
But I won't stop myself with regret because it leaves a bad taste in my mouth. So I reach for water to wash it down. I sip the memory slowly down my throat. Gone forever once more.
You, who I once knew in the *sandy* light of the sun when I was twenty-one and in love.
Maryland's eastern shores know all of our secrets, and maybe Gino does too.
Between the three of us, it was bound to be true!

The season changed in your mind, the seasons changed outside. Summer was our time and it would never be the same. Choosing was never your choice. One hand was holding your spite for your father's approval, the other was holding my heart.
We both know that you would never have married her if I had played the game—
Oh and I would have been good at it too. What if, What if, What if.
What if I had stayed?
What if I had driven to you?
What if you ran away with me?
For you, I would have cheated to win. Nothing would have stopped me for your love.

Yet I am the loser in this game.
My king taken, my cards folded.
Defeat turned to a longing I had never
Known. The turn of a chapter.
The coming of age through pain.
An old friend that visits me often.
I left to save myself. I got out of that not-so merry land and flew.
If self-sabotage was the reward in heaven for preservation, I would be in paradise by now.
Unfortunately it's not, so hell clings to my lips where you once were.
That season hits harder than reality every year. I'm older now, and those days have come and gone.
Only now you're the phantom lover that I put my red lipstick on for.
Gino was right.

The summer has set low beneath the skies of our love.
Where are you these days?
Do you sit in a room with people you never cared for only to dream of me too?
Are you upstairs in Erik's attic still?
I want to know…but I can't.

Me? I'm still there wading my feet in the cool salt water of Assateague,
Twenty-one catching a cold from the heartache left by time.
The sweats in the night tell me I'm trying to break the fever of you—

Prognosis says I never will though
Here I am with our season coming to another end.

How long? I ask myself,

Will our season haunt me until death do us part?

Light of My Life

How softly the light
From the window touches me.

The only early morning lover that has ever stayed.

She wisps between my fingers,
Caresses my face,
And warms my heart.

If she ever does leave
I know she'll always come back.
She's promised to me, but I'm not promised to her.
This is written in the stars.

For what it's worth,
I know this is the hope I want
To stay in forever.

The light of my life.

Moon to Me

If I could bring life to the moon
I'd move there with you
Where we would
Live together in harmony
Just you and me
Lightyears away
For all the stars to see.
Why?
Because you are the Moon to Me.

Trees

That's when I look up to the trees
And I say to myself,
When will I be twenty foot three?
Seeing high above the sky
Waiving my branches for all to see.

I envy the roots
And scamper to touch the bark
Only to know their truth.
Because what is it that you know?
Tell me all the things I don't.

That's when I look up to the trees
Picking their green leaves
Hating the ground I touch
Just wanting to feel the breeze.

Because down here
Ain't no one who can breathe.
I hear symphonies with these trees.
Every time the wind blows,
The wood pulls like strings
Making notes of A or maybe G.
In their own right, they sing.

I could sit staring,
Sit listening,
Sit speaking
Words of wishes to these beings
Because that's when I'm most myself:
When I'm looking up at the trees.

Re: Nothing

What do I know about nothing?
It's harsh, it's cold.
It leaves you wanting.
But let me tell you something: Nothing is flat and leaves you small.
Nothing is no good at all. But you tell me I have nothing to share.
What do I know about nothing?
 I know more than I can bear.

A Motet to Fear

These rooms feel the same
Empty in design
Then there's you
Always on my mind.

Cold to the touch,
You turn away
Long live the dead
Knowing the living can't stay.

A love that never was
Dead from the start
Now here I stand
Without a heart

Walking away
You were scared,
Fearful of me
Knowing you erred.

So go now,
Run for the hills
I'll bleed out
Whispering the words,
"I love you still."

Little Long Hair

Little Long Hair of mine, the brown streaks shine in the light.
I think it's cute that there are grays that whisper among the others.
But I don't mind
They belong. They always have. They always will.
They were destined for that spot on my head and I refuse to pluck them.

This hair of mine is so beautiful and if someday it falls out I will cry.
It's the only thing I could control and love without judgment.
The only friend I had that never left me behind.

Each night I play with it, softly stroking its layers.
Papa and Mama gave me this beautiful hair.
Not even my sister has hair like this.

I am the Samson of our family.
Lord bring me no Delilah, for I could not endure any cutting of my power.
Little long hair, I would die happily tied to pillars with chains
If you stayed sticky with blood on my head until the very end.
If that's what it took,
I would.

Little Long Hair of mine.

Hot Springs

Have you ever driven miles away to another state, just to cry yourself to sleep?
I left letters somewhere he'll never read. Deep in the forest is a bottle of whiskey he gave me. *Sheepdog* has the words I could never say, and the ground below is well watered with the taste of peanut butter and alcohol that if the trees themselves could walk they would only sway.

Have you ever given yourself so fully to someone only to have them throw you away?
I cried in front of St. Mary's, thinking, *Why did you make me this way?* A cruel irony for someone so young is the want to be loved, yet made to be so high strung.

Have you ever seen Hot Springs in the cold? When the sun shined I screamed real
bold. Only the lake heard me. She whimpered against the shore at my feet with her waves. I knew she knew I wanted to stay. Happiness is the song I heard as I gazed into the naked trees.
But happiness would take years just to find me.

Now the seasons have come and gone since that time. You should know that Hot Springs is where I left all the memories that once were mine.

Even when things seem normal, just when things seems fine, I can't help but question:

Have you ever wanted to ask them what could have been different if everything went right?

Lightning Source UK Ltd.
Milton Keynes UK
UKHW010938081221
395308UK00010B/1184